Date: 3/27/14

BR 796.323 NEL
Nelson, Robin,
Basketball is fun! /

Basketball Is Fun!

by Robin Nelson

first step nonfiction

Lerner Publications Company · Minneapolis

LERNER

Expand learning beyond the printed book. Download free, complementary educational resources for this book from our website, www.lerneresource.com.

SOURCE™

The images in this book are used with the permission of: © iStockphoto.com/Hilary Brodey, p. 4; © iStockphoto.com/Christopher Futcher, pp. 5, 7, 13; © Alfred Abad/age fotostock/SuperStock, p. 6; © iStockphoto.com/Matthew Brown, p. 8; © iStockphoto.com/Chad Truemper, p. 9; © Serge Kozak/CORBIS, pp. 10, 11; © Tom & Dee Ann McCarthy/CORBIS, p. 12; © iStockphoto.com/Rob Friedman, pp. 14, 15, 16, 18; © William Saliaz/CORBIS, p. 17; © iStockphoto.com/Bill Grove, p. 19.

Front cover: © iStockphoto.com/Mark Herreid.

Main body text set in ITC Avant Garde Gothic Std Medium 21/25.
Typeface provided by Adobe Systems.

Lerner Publications Company
A division of Lerner Publishing Group, Inc.
241 First Avenue North
Minneapolis, MN 55401 U.S.A.

Website address: www.lernerbooks.com

Library of Congress Cataloging-in-Publication Data

Nelson, Robin, 1971–
    Basketball is fun! / by Robin Nelson.
       p.   cm. — (First step nonfiction—sports are fun!)
    Includes index.
    ISBN 978–1–4677–1102–9 (lib. bdg. : alk. paper)
    ISBN 978–1–4677–1744–1 (eBook)
    1. Baseball—Juvenile literature. I. Title.
  GV867.5.N455 2014
  796.323—dc23   2012041523

Manufactured in the United States of America
1 – PC – 7/15/13

Table of Contents

Do you like to shoot **baskets**?

You can play basketball!

Two teams play basketball.

The team that makes the
most baskets wins.

You need a ball to play basketball.

8

You need a basket. You
throw the ball into a basket
to score.

Shoot and Score

The game starts in the middle of the **court**.

The **referee** throws the ball into the air.

The players try to **tip** the
ball to their team.

The team that gets the tip
tries to get close to their
basket.

Players **dribble** the ball down the court.

A player passes the ball to
a **teammate**.

He takes a shot at the basket.

He misses.

His teammate gets the ball
and shoots.

It goes in! He made a basket.

The Basketball Court

A basketball court can be inside or outside. The court has a basket at each end.

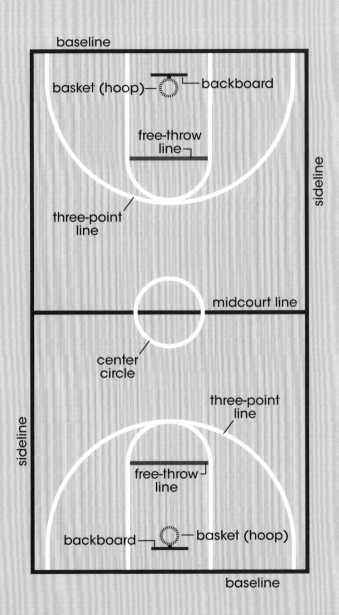

baseline

basket (hoop) — backboard

free-throw line

three-point line

midcourt line

center circle

three-point line

free-throw line

backboard — basket (hoop)

sideline

sideline

baseline

Fun Facts

- A team usually gets two points for scoring a basket. If a team makes a basket from outside the three-point line, the team gets three points.

- If someone breaks a rule, a player on the other team might get an extra chance to shoot a basket. If the shooter makes a basket, he gets one point.

- Basketball is a great way to get exercise!

Glossary

baskets – when the ball goes into the basket in basketball. *Basket* is also the name for the net in basketball.

court – a rectangular-shaped surface used for playing basketball

dribble – to move the ball forward by bouncing it

referee – a person who makes sure the players are following the rules

teammate – a person who is on the same team

tip – push

Index